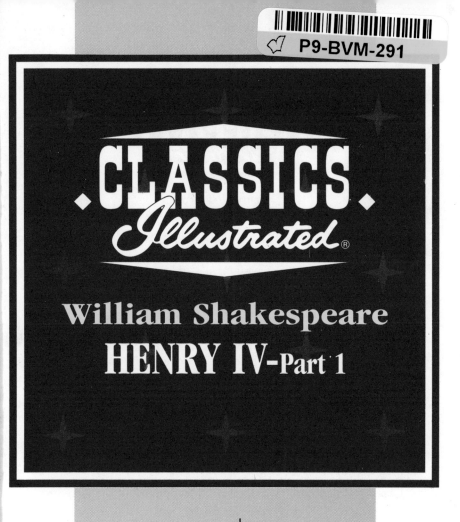

CLASSICS Illustrated®

William Shakespeare
HENRY IV-Part 1

essay by
Susan Shwartz, Ph.D.

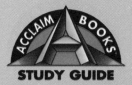

ACCLAIM BOOKS
STUDY GUIDE

Henry IV-Part 1
A Classics Illustrated Original Edition

Art by Patrick Broderick
Adaption by Gregory Feeley
Cover by George Pratt

For Classics Illustrated Study Guides
computer coloring by Twilight Graphics
editor: Madeleine Robins
assistant editor: Valerie D'Orazio
design: Joseph Caponsacco

Classics Illustrated: Henry IV-Part 1 © Twin Circle Publishing Co.,
a division of Frawley Enterprises; licensed to First Classics, Inc. All new
material and compilation © 1998 by Acclaim Books, Inc.

Dale-Chall R.L.: 9.3
ISBN 1-57840-187-9

Classics Illustrated® is a registered trademark of the Frawley
Corporation.

Acclaim Books, New York, NY
Printed in the United States

LONDON, 1402. WITH THE WEAK KING RICHARD II DEPOSED, HENRY BOLINGBROKE IS NOW KING OF ENGLAND. BUT THE CIVIL STRIFE THAT HAS TORN THE REALM WILL NOT HEAL SO EASILY...

HENRY IV
PART 1
BY
WILLIAM SHAKESPEARE

SO SHAKEN AS WE ARE, SO WAN WITH CARE, FIND WE A TIME FOR FRIGHTED PEACE TO PANT AND BREATHE SHORTWINDED ACCENTS OF NEW BROILS TO BE COMMENCED IN STRONDS AFAR REMOTE. NO MORE THE THIRSTY ENTRANCE OF THIS SOIL SHALL DAUB HER LIPS WITH HER OWN CHILDREN'S BLOOD...

"NO MORE SHALL TRENCHING WAR CHANNEL HER FIELDS, NOR BRUISE HER FLOW'RETS WITH THE ARMED HOOFS OF HOSTILE PACES. THOSE OPPOSED EYES WHICH, LIKE THE METEORS OF A TROUBLED HEAVEN, DID LATELY MEET IN THE INTESTINE SHOCK AND FURIOUS CLOSE OF CIVIL BUTCHERY--
--SHALL NOW IN MUTUAL WELL BESEEMING RANKS MARCH ALL ONE WAY AND BE NO MORE OPPOSED AGAINST ACQUAINTANCE, KINDRED, AND ALLIES. THE EDGE OF WAR, LIKE AN ILL-SHEATHED KNIFE, NO MORE SHALL CUT ITS MASTER."
"THEREFORE, FRIENDS, AS FAR AS TO THE SEPULCHER OF CHRIST--WHOSE SOLDIER NOW, UNDER WHOSE BLESSED CROSS WE ARE IMPRESSED AND ENGAGED TO FIGHT-- FORTHWITH A POWER OF ENGLISH SHALL WE LEVY, TO CHASE THESE PAGANS IN THOSE HOLY FIELDS OVER WHOSE ACRES WALKED THOSE BLESSED FEET WHICH FOURTEEN HUNDRED YEARS AGO WERE NAILED FOR OUR ADVANTAGE ON THE BITTER CROSS."
"BUT THIS OUR PURPOSE IS NOW TWELVEMONTH OLD, AND BOOTLESS 'TIS TO TELL YOU WE WILL GO. THEREFOR WE MEET NOT NOW. THEN LET ME HEAR OF YOU, MY GENTLE COUSIN WESTMORELAND, WHAT YESTERNIGHT OUR COUNCIL DID DECREE IN FORWARDING THIS DEAR EXPEDIENCE."

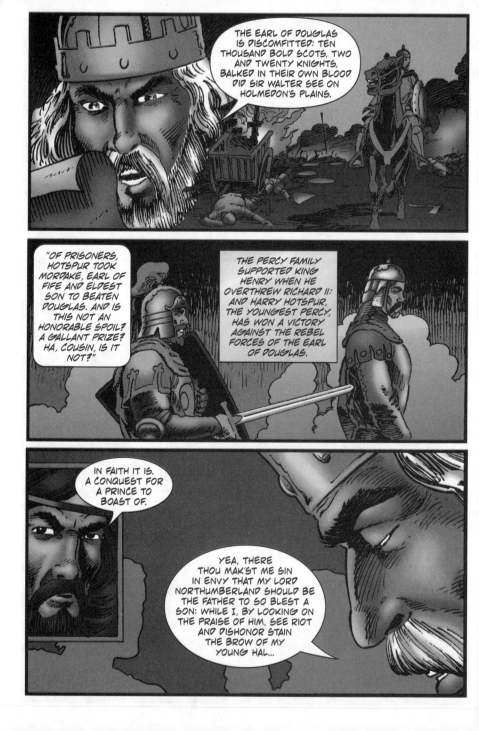

DRAMATIS PERSONAE

KING HENRY IV (HENRY BOLINGBROKE) DEPOSED RICHARD II BEFORE THE START OF THE PLAY.

PRINCE JOHN OF LANCASTER THE KING'S YOUNGEST SON.

PRINCE HAL (HARRY MONMOUTH) THE PRINCE OF WALES, AND HEIR TO THE THRONE.

THE EARL OF WESTMORELAND KING HENRY'S PRIMARY ADVISOR.

SIR WALTER BLUNT ONE OF THE KING'S KNIGHTS.

OWEN GLENDOWER A WELSH REBEL, MORTIMER'S IN-LAW.

THOMAS PERCY, EARL OF WORCESTER A FORMER ALLY OF THE KING.

HENRY PERCY, EARL OF NORTHUMBERLAND ANOTHER FORMER ALLY, WORCESTER'S BROTHER.

EDMUND MORTIMER RICHARD II'S RIGHTFUL HEIR.

EARL OF DOUGLAS A SCOTTISH REBEL.

KATE HOTSPUR'S WIFE.

HENRY PERCY ("HOTSPUR") NORTHUMBER-LAND'S SON.

NED POINS A FRIEND OF HAL'S.

SIR JOHN FALSTAFF A RIOTOUS KNIGHT.

PETO.

MISTRESS QUICKLY HOSTESS TO THE TAVERN.

BARDOLPH.

GADSHILL.

THREE MEMBERS OF FALSTAFF'S GANG.

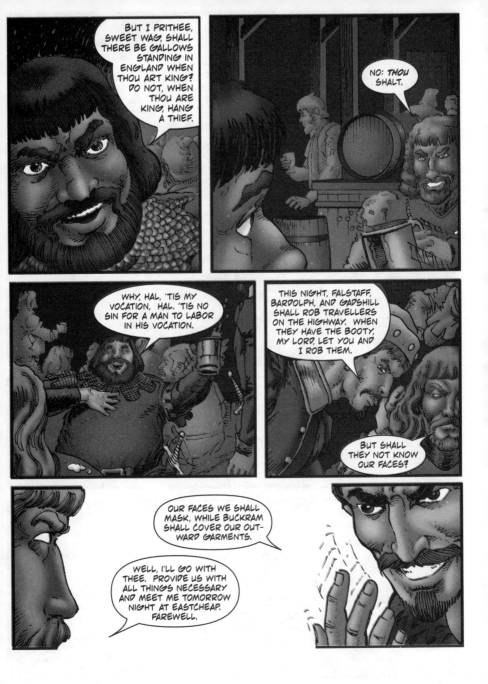

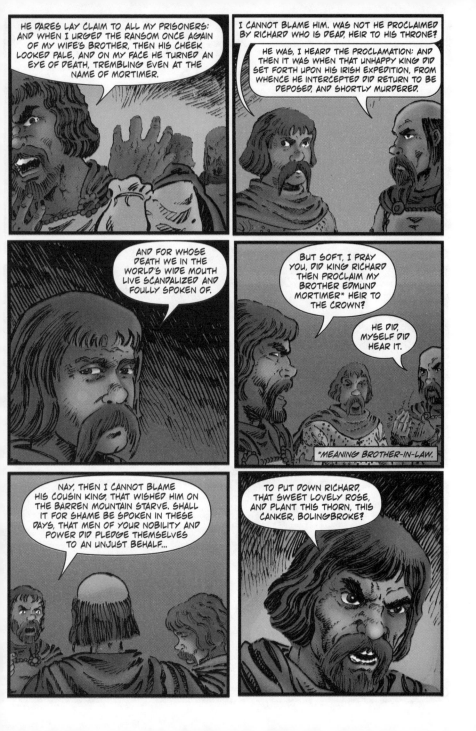

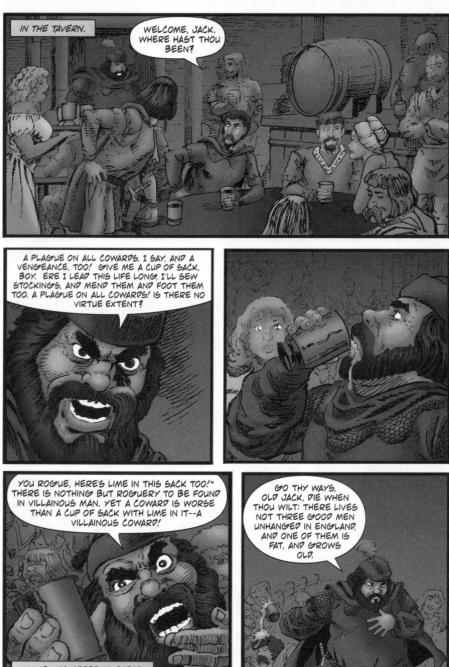

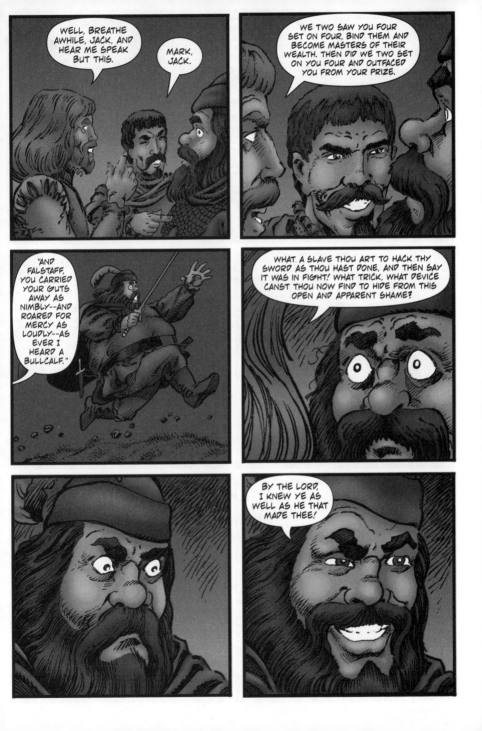

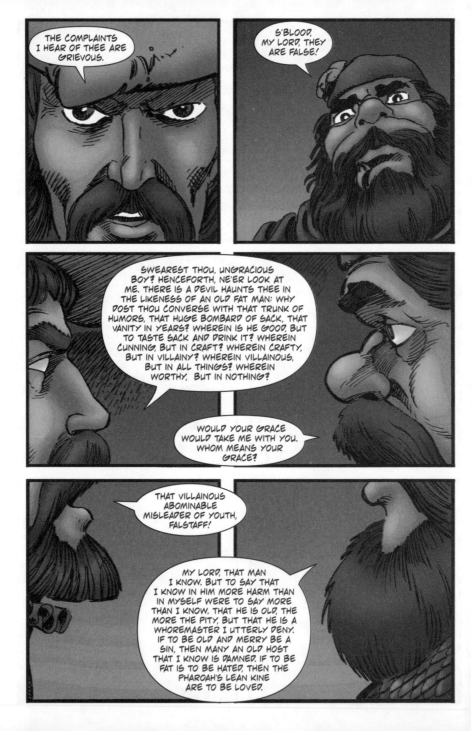

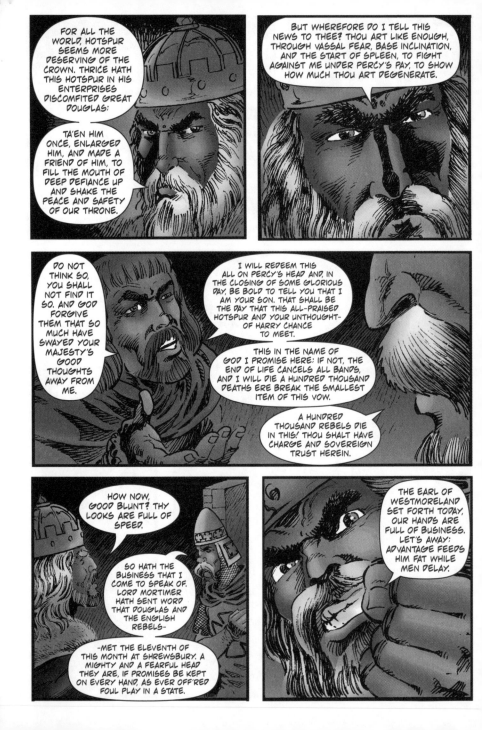

O HARRY, THOU HAST ROBBED ME OF MY YOUTH! I BETTER BROOK THE LOSS OF BRITTLE LIFE THAN THOSE PROUD TITLES THOU HAST WON OF ME. THEY WOUND MY THOUGHTS WORSE THAN THY SWORD MY FLESH.

HENRY IV-Part 1

William Shakespeare

History professors often lament that you can't learn English history by reading Shakespeare's history plays. At the same time, English history, and history as created by Shakespeare, are a part of British tradition that permeates the awareness of educated English-speakers. So in discussing what are called the "Wars of the Roses" you must remember that Shakespeare's history plays are a nexus, or connection point, where historical fact and historical myth coexist.

in rooms in London, owned shares in a prominent theater, managed to get himself in trouble in the country before traveling to London where political trouble sometimes found him, who didn't find a lawsuit or two at all amiss, and who wrote plays that have managed to enter the English language as classics, often produced and quoted so often that you may not be aware that you're quoting Shakespeare.

The parish church of Holy Trinity records the baptism on April 26, 1564, of William Shakespeare in Stratford-upon-Avon, in Warwickshire, some 85 miles northwest of London. No record of his birth survives, although it's usually celebrated on April 23, because that is the day of England's patron Saint George—and of Shakespeare's death in 1616.

His father John, born to tenant farmers, was an ambitious man. In an age of expansion, he rose to own his own glover's shop and to become bailiff of Stratford, a position similar to mayor. He married Mary Arden, of slightly better birth than he and an heiress, and bought two houses. In about 1576, he applied to the Office of Heralds for the right to be called gentleman; this meant, among other

THE AUTHOR

Today, when William Shakespeare as Cultural Icon has almost crowded out Shakespeare as writer, it may take a commercial writer to point out that Shakespeare managed to achieve every writer's dream. Not only did he travel to the big city to make his fortune, he worked at what he loved, succeeded at it financially, in the praise of his audience, and the respect of his colleagues. He rose in the world and retired, a well-off man, back to his home town.

Let's look at the writer, who lived

things, that he would be granted a coat of arms. Although this petition went nowhere at the time, because of what sounds like a bad run of financial and political luck, William Shakespeare subsequently saw his father's dream through. It is reflected in his writing; *The Winter's Tale*, one of his very last plays, has a funny scene in which a clown and a shepherd joke about being "gentlemen born," albeit only for four hours so far.

This idea of coats of arms and heraldry is important in the History Plays. Coats of arms are the emblems worn by gentlemen, nobles and royalty, unique markings that identify a given man, his family, and his achievements. There are extremely strict rules for how they may be combined and to whom arms may be awarded. So Shakespeare, in carrying out his father's dream, was actually participating in the history that was simultaneously his source, his experience, and his subject matter.

Shakespeare grew up as the eldest child, with three younger brothers and two younger sisters, a solidly middle-class family in an unwalled medieval town. As befitted solid citizens during Elizabeth's reign, the Shakespeares were members of the Church of England, and lived through the wars against Spain (they would have been part of the nationwide rejoicing when the Spanish Armada was destroyed in

1588, for example). He attended the Stratford grammar school, where he chiefly learned Latin—so much for "little Latin and less Greek"—but not Oxford or Cambridge University like other leading playwrights of his day, such as Ben Jonson.

He probably learned much from his surroundings—the forests, the River Avon, market days, and a fair for which Stratford was famous in the region. This love of nature shows in his evocation of the English countryside—somewhat in *Henry IV, Part I*, but far more in *Henry IV, Part II*.

As a mercantile town, Stratford drew companies of actors that put on performances at the guildhall. By the time Shakespeare was a youth, he had probably seen plays put on by the Earl of Warwick's men, the Earl of Worcester's men, and the Earl of Leicester's men. This last was England's leading adult company, whose patron was the Earl of Leicester, and whose principal artist was the James Burbage who built the first theater in London and became the father of the great actor Richard Burbage, Shakespeare's colleague and friend. Note the names of these patrons of theatre companies; they are the names of great lords of the History Plays, who no doubt felt a vested interest in the deeds of their ancestors.

Shakespeare married young, in 1582, to Anne Hathaway of Stratford, who was eight years older than he and who gave birth to his eldest child

Susanna on May 26, 1583. William and Anne had two other children, twins—Judith and Hamnet, baptized February 2, 1585.

By 1592, Shakespeare had moved to London to make his fortune as actor, playwright, and share owner in a theatrical company. Many writers who move to the big city are told "don't give up your day job." Shakespeare's day job was the thing he loved. He made a considerable impression early on and drew the fire of less-successful literary men such as Robert Greene, who complained about an "upstart crow…with a Tiger's heart wrapped in a player's hide…" who dared to believe himself the only "Shake-scene" in the country. Such writers resented not only his popularity but his lack of a university degree.

In London, Shakespeare was able to live in a city much larger than his native Stratford. Elizabeth's London was, above all things, alive—a city filled with history, turmoil, and politics—the very subject and site of the History Plays. No doubt, between performances and writing marathons, Shakespeare had a chance to talk with soldiers and sailors, actors, and nobles. No doubt he stayed up nights in taverns drinking (how else could he have created Falstaff?), hearing old battle stories and new stories of the New World, all of which went into his plays. No doubt, he saw the heads of traitors exhibited on London Bridge.

But Shakespeare didn't just listen to the rough-and-tumble crowd. Like his father, he had an eye to advancement, which meant important patrons. By 1594, Shakespeare had also become distinguished as a poet—elaborate, sophisticated verse that won him the praise of young noblemen—as well as a playwright.

His output is relatively small—some 37 plays plus several, like *Two Noble Kinsmen*, which are collaborations—plus his sonnet cycle and several long, secular poems. But he prospered from them and became well known. *Merry Wives of Windsor* was written in obedience to Queen Elizabeth, who wanted to see "Falstaff (who makes his appearance in *Henry IV, Part I*) in love." (You might wish to note that, in happier times, when Diana, Princess of Wales, and Sarah, Duchess of York, had not been divorced and were cheerfully going to nightclubs and races, one columnist referred to them as "the merry wives of Windsor," a reference to the current ruling dynasty as well as to Windsor Castle, from which it takes its name.)

A Queen's notice could be tricky, however, especially in the matter of the history plays. A production of *Richard II* almost backfired upon Shakespeare because the play, like the story itself, deals with the overthrow of a king by the man who became Henry IV.

In 1596, Shakespeare's son Hamnet died. Also in that year, ironically enough, Shakespeare achieved his father's dream of a coat of arms: he was a gentleman now, but without an heir. Nevertheless, he kept on. In

1599, he was listed as a shareholder in the newly constructed Globe Theater; and was arguably the most popular playwright in the City.

In 1603, Queen Elizabeth died; King James I ultimately took over Shakespeare's company, which became known as the King's Men. From 1598 to 1609, he wrote some of his finest plays, among them *As You Like It, Henry V, Julius Caesar, Othello, Hamlet*, and *Much Ado About Nothing*.

No doubt Shakespeare divided his time between London and Stratford, where he retired and where he died in 1616. He was buried as "Will. Shakspere, gent." within the parish church, with a rhyme on his headstone cursing anyone who disturbed his bones—which have, as a matter of fact, never been touched.

He lived to see his grandchildren and to be acclaimed as a playwright and as a gentleman. In 1623, old friends and actors John Heminge and Henry Condell cooperated with the London stationers in publishing a collected edition of his plays, complete with pictures and an ode by the poet and playwright Ben Jonson, who hailed him as "not of an age, but for all time."

Jonson never wrote a better line.

BACKGROUND

As the eminent Shakespearean scholar Alfred Harbage pointed out,

the eight history plays from *Richard II* to *Richard III* provide an overview of the period from 1398 to 1485 "when modern England was being born." This period is often called the Wars of the Roses, from the emblems taken by the two offshoots of the Plantagenet dynasty that began to rule England in the twelfth century with Henry II. The white rose was an emblem of the Yorkists, descendants of the Duke of York, and the red roses were an emblem of the Lancastrians, descendants of John of Gaunt, Duke of Lancaster. The break begins with Richard II, grandson of Edward III, who was deposed by Henry, son of John of Gaunt. Quarrels over who was the rightful holder of the English throne created almost a century of civil strife (on top of the Hundred Years' War with France, in which England lost what Henry V gained at Agincourt), and, ultimately, cost the Plantagenets the throne when Henry VII, son of Owen Tudor and Henry V's widow, married Elizabeth of York after defeating Richard III of the Plantagenets.

Thus, the Plantagenets were replaced by the Tudors; subsequent dynasties—and the Commonwealth of Oliver Cromwell and his son, as Lords Protector—have succeeded them. Today's Queen, Elizabeth II of the Windsor Dynasty, is 42nd in line from William the Conqueror, who took the throne in 1066.

In *Henry IV, Part I*, we see several aspects of this struggle. The Mortimer family allies with the

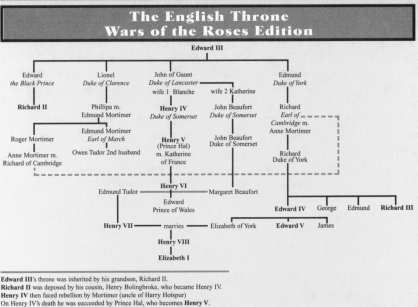

Welsh, long-time enemies to the "Southrons" because they claim the throne as rightful heirs to Richard II, who died without a son. Henry IV is tormented by guilt and he wishes to atone by going on Crusade—although the great age of the cru-

sading movement (which began in 1095) is long past. And Henry's son, Prince Hal, who will become the warrior hero Henry V, will pray at Agincourt not to be punished for his father's crimes. The problem, is simple: one can't truly repent without giving up the thing for which one performed the crime. As much as King Henry IV

feels guilty for seizing the throne, he remains king. Richard II died while imprisoned; and the remaining century of dynastic wars works itself out as a kind of retribution until all is resolved in the induction of Henry VII, the reign of Henry VIII, and the prophecy of the triumph of Queen Elizabeth I.

Like the action of *Henry IV, Part I*, which follows closely after the death of King Richard II, the plays follow each other in order of composition. *Richard II* was written by 1596, and scholars assign 1597 as the composition date for *Henry IV, Part I*.

Like most of the other history plays, *Henry IV* is drawn from

Holinshed's *Chronicles* as well as the earlier chronicle of Hall. Shakespeare also used as a source Samuel Daniel's poem *The Civil Wars* (1595), which pits Prince Hal against Hotspur and stresses his role at the Battle of Shrewsbury (on the Welsh border), which forms the military climax of this play. It isn't new ground to English drama; an old play called *The Famous Victories of Henry V* had already used the highway-robber episode at Gad's Hill and taken the story all the way to Henry V's marriage.

It is important to remember, of course, that Shakespeare was writing drama, not history, and makes no bones about changing events or characters to make them more dramatic. Sometimes, too, he is dead wrong: for example, in *Richard II*, he follows Holinshed's confusion of Sir Edmund Mortimer, who married the daughter of Owen Glendower, with Edmund Mortimer, whom King Richard named as heir in 1398. Furthermore, like the chroniclers of his day—and nowhere more so than in *Richard III*—Shakespeare sides with the winners, who do indeed get to write official history. Such chroniclers are partisan and not above what we would today call revisionism—shading facts in order to go along with the prevailing ideology. In Shakespeare's case, the winner was Elizabeth I, a powerful and intelligent monarch indeed and one well aware of the power of the play or, as we might say today, of the power of the media.

But it is wrong to call Shakespeare a mere propagandist. As a popular writer, he indeed had patrons to please and a Queen whose favor he needed to keep; as an extraordinarily gifted writer, he took these flawed bits of history and error and melded them into a kind of truth that, since his day, has helped England define itself as "This blessed plot, this earth, this realm, this England" (*Richard II*) and declare its ability to stand fast, as proclaimed in the much earlier play, *King John*: "Come the three corners of the world in arms/And we shall shock them. Nought shall make us rue/ If England to itself do rest but true."

These were the plays that formed Sir Winston Churchill's early reading and his mindset, and enabled him to inspire the English people during the Battle of Britain in World War II, during which, it isn't an exaggeration to say, Shakespeare's verse joined Churchill's prose ("this was their finest hour") as not-so-secret weapons against the Axis powers.

Traditions springing from Shakespeare's time (and Henry IV's) continue in our time, very often in moments of pageantry or crisis.

For example, Prince Charles learned Welsh and was made Prince of Wales in Caernarvon, kneeling before his mother the Queen to take his oath. Following the example of their father the Prince Consort, Prince Charles and Prince Andrew both served in the British Navy, and Prince Andrew saw action in the Falkland

Islands as a helicopter pilot. The newest generation of princes are William and Harry, after several English kings, including, of course, Prince Hal in this play.

Most recently, if you watched the funeral for Diana, Princess of Wales, you saw that the old devices are still in use. Diana's coffin was covered with the royal crest and a spray of lilies. Although, as commentators pointed out, Diana's "device" was the lily; Elton John sang of her in Westminster Abbey (the construction of which was begun by Henry III and in which Henry V is buried) as "England's Rose." This is the tradition that has passed into popular culture, and the one upon which he drew.

CHARACTERS

King Henry IV (Lancaster)

Henry IV still shows the strength and focus that made him, as Bolingbroke in *Richard II*, able to win people's respect and, ultimately, take the throne from Richard—but he is a man for whom time is running out,

and he knows it. Though remaining very much in control of the kingdom he acquired, Henry is torn between his desire to atone for his

takeover by going on a Crusade, and his desire to keep the kingdom secure against more wars of succession and threats from the Welsh. He is a good administrator and a good fighter, if not as good as he has been; he envies Hotspur (Harry Percy) because he reminds him of himself and how well he was regarded as a young man. And his sorrow is that his own son isn't more like Percy and himself. Though he is a king, this is a disappointed and tormented man.

Henry of Monmouth, Prince of Wales (Prince Hal)

The Prince of Wales plays two roles in this play. As Prince Hal, he is a gamester, a trickster, who acts like a ne'er-do-well, the better to impress people when he ultimately does come to power. In that he is able to resist Falstaff's appeal, he shows that he has the type of self-control needed for the warrior-king he is to become: still, this is a somewhat dubious strategy that is made palatable only by the strength of the language and the actor speaking the lines.

In his dealings with Falstaff and with the Eastcheap (a business district in the East of London) characters, Prince Hal does seem to enjoy himself. Note that he himself doesn't turn robber; he attacks Falstaff. He manages to win these people's loyalty and even seems to like them, but, at the same time, he knows them for what they are and sometimes, even as he plays along, you can see him thinking about what he's planning to do next. This tricky, manipulative use of people makes him very much his father's son. Yet, at the same time, his high spirits make him attractive. And his courage on the field of battle (historical note: Prince Hal was only sixteen at the time) prepares the reader—or audience—for his future glory as the victor of Agincourt.

Prince John of Lancaster (brother to Prince Hal)

Prince John is a secondary character portrayed in a few lines and scenes as precisely what he should be: honorable, brave, and loyal.

Earl of Westmoreland

One of the great magnates of England, here serving as an "attendant lord."

Sir Walter Blunt

The name, although a historical one, speaks for itself. Sir Walter is a brave and loyal knight who dies on the battlefield, disguised as the man he serves.

REVOLTED MORTIMER? HE NEVER DID FALL OFF, MY SOVEREIGN LIEGE. BUT BY THE CHANCE OF WAR. TO PROVE THAT TRUE HE DID ENGAGE THE BEST PART OF AN HOUR IN CHARGING HARDIMENT WITH GREAT GLENDOWER. SO LET HIM NOT BE SLANDERED WITH REVOLT.

Thomas Percy, Earl of Worcester

Another of the great lords of England and part of a very noble Northern family, Worcester trades sides. He is a very crafty, proud man who is able to mobilize his powerful family.

Harry Percy, Earl of Northumberland

Another of the great Northern lords, Percy is a fighting earl and very proud. The distinction Shakespeare draws between up-country and low-landers makes him appear less polished than the Southern earls: this is probably deliberate.

Henry Percy (Hotspur), son of Earl of Northumberland

One of the finest fighting men of his days, Harry Percy is well-nicknamed Hotspur. He is proud, rash, and funny, deeply devoted to his wife, and almost catastrophically impulsive. You could never imagine him, like Prince Hal, playing a part; in fact, his dealings with Owen Glendower show Harry impatient of dreams and pretensions, although he himself can embark on flights of fancy. Although charming and brave, he isn't precisely stable enough—and far too easily distracted—to be king. Shakespeare portrays him and Prince Hal as being agemates: at the Battle of Shrewsbury, however, Hotspur was actually 39.

Edmund Mortimer, Earl of March

Not much appears of March in the adaptation of this play. In the actual text, he is shown as a very young man, sentimentally attached to Glendower's daughter, who speaks no English (as he speaks no Welsh).

Richard Scroop, Archbishop of York

Of a noble family, the Archbishop of York holds one of the two most powerful bishoprics in England (the only one more powerful and more venerable is Canterbury). Men like this Archbishop are the sorts of people best described by the title "prince of the Church." They almost regard their bishoprics as if they were fiefdoms and prove to be skillful politicians.

I AM ACCURSED TO ROB IN THAT THIEF'S COMPANY. THE RASCAL HATH REMOVED MY HORSE AND TIED IT I KNOW NOT WHERE. POINS! HAL! A PLAGUE UPON IT WHEN THIEVES CANNOT BE TRUE TO ONE ANOTHER!

Archibald, Earl of Douglas

He is a highlander earl, very proud, very fierce, and very determined, and an ally to the Percy clan.

Owen Glendower (Welsh rebel)

In actual history, Glendower was a charismatic figure and powerful rebel who claimed descent from King Arthur and, after being defeated, vanished into the hills, allegedly—again like Arthur—to return at need. He drew the Welsh bards about him and wrapped himself in the political and bardic prophecies that people put a lot of faith in at that time, to such an extent that Henry IV outlawed them. Some hints of that remain in Shakespeare's portrayal of an egocentric and almost crazy visionary, whose verbal jousts with Hotspur about signs and portents are part of the comic action of the play.

Sir John Falstaff

In the creation of Falstaff, Shakespeare had two sources—Sir John Fastolfe and Sir John Oldcastle, but he departed from both in order to create a character who has become a synonym for riotous good cheer. In some ways, he is a natural phenomenon—from his immense, drink-reddened nose to his even huger belly. He is a creature of appetites and an unabashed coward and liar in an era that made much of pride and honor. It is a tribute to his humor and his inventiveness that he also wins the immense affection that he does. This is one of the great characters in literature, who almost steals the play and, ultimately, walks out of it into literature at large. In him, Shakespeare indulges his mastery of language: Falstaff can twist the language to make it anything he wishes, and he is as verbally and mentally nimble as he is physically lazy. Unfortunately for him, it is a brilliance without control.

He appears in several others of Shakespeare's works, notably *Henry IV, part II*, and *Henry V* (offstage and sadly), and also in *The Merry Wives of Windsor*, which was written to gratify Queen Elizabeth. Verdi put him in an opera; Orson Welles's *Chimes at Midnight* portrays him at his best as a kind of lord of Misrule who turns tragic; and he is a "type" or example of a certain sort of character who appears in many different forms in many different texts. Science fiction author Poul Anderson's Nicholas van

Rijn is a Falstaffian character as is Harcourt Fenton (Harry) Mudd, who appears in several classic *Star Trek* episodes.

Poins

Ned, or Edward, Poins is one of the hangers-on to Falstaff, and the one who stands close to the Prince. Somewhat better-bred than the others, he is the man who suggests the highway robbery trick against Falstaff. He is able enough to carry out such an elaborate practical joke and to win some of Prince Hal's affection. He has a nasty temper.

Peto
Bardolph, vintner of a tavern in Eastcheap
Francis, a waiter

These are some of Shakespeare's comic figures, drawn broadly and perceptively. Bardolph, especially, is a continuing character and notable for his nose and his alcoholism.

Lady Percy (Hotspur's wife and Mortimer's sister)

In the unabridged play, Lady Percy is passionately in love with her husband and almost as fierce and funny as he is.

Lady Mortimer, Glendower's daughter

In the unabridged play, if Lady Percy is all fire, Lady Mortimer is sentimental and plays a farewell on her Welsh harp.

Mistress Quickly, hostess of an Eastcheap tavern

Mistress Quickly is another character who continues throughout the histories. Ribald, humorous, not nearly as young as she used to be or as virtuous as she should be, she nevertheless makes a sort of home in Eastcheap for Falstaff and his friends, and wins a kind of fondness from Prince Hal. Like the Nurse in *Romeo and Juliet* or the Wife of Bath in Chaucer's *Canterbury Tales*, Mistress Quickly is a splendid comic portrayal of a woman of low degree but high vitality and enthusiasm.

THE STORY

The History of King Henry IV opens with the king telling one of his younger sons, John of Lancaster, the Earl of Westmoreland, and several others to go "as far as to the sepulchre of Christ," a reference to the medieval custom of going on Crusade, a long-cherished ambition of Henry IV's. His desire to leave England to seek Jerusalem is thwarted by Westmoreland's accounts of battles by Mortimer against Owen Glendower, a

Welsh nationalist who captures the man whom some believe is England's rightful king. Westmoreland also tells of a

battle at Holmedon in which Harry Percy, son of the Earl of Northumberland, performed many brave deeds. Henry is extremely envious of the Earl; his own heir, Prince Hal, isn't living up to his father's expectations ("I…See riot and dishonor stain the brow/Of my young Harry."). At the same time, Hotspur refuses to send the King all of the prisoners whom he has taken and whom, as a proper vassal, he should send on.

In Act I, scene ii, the scene shifts. Here we see the Prince of Wales drinking and talking rather fantastically in an Eastcheap tavern with Sir John Falstaff, the immensely fat, jovial, and cowardly lowlife with whom he has taken up. Falstaff, always short of money, actually agrees—or pretends to agree—to rob some travelers on the road to Canterbury.

Other men enter; one of them, Ned Poins, suggests that he and Prince Hal put on disguises and attack Falstaff at Gad's Hill and give him the fright of his life. Prince Hal likes this idea. After all the others have left, Hal's speech ("I know you all…") declares his intention of hiding like "the base contagious cloud" behind his low-life companions, only to emerge "like bright metal in a sullen ground."

In Act I, scene iii, the King rebukes Hotspur, Northumberland,

and Worcester, who quarrel with him. The King orders them to send him their prisoners and leaves, whereupon Hotspur indulges in a flight of fancy in which mixed images of the current heir, Henry IV's overthrow of Richard II, and many other "wild and whirling words" (to borrow a line from *Hamlet*) combine to show his emotionality and his rage. England is well on its way to civil war, as the Northerners break with the lowlanders.

Act II returns us to Eastcheap. A train of merchants is preparing to ride out. Falstaff is fretting, all the more so because Ned Poins has hidden his horse, forcing the fat old knight to walk. Poins and Prince Hal assume their disguises and, after Falstaff attacks the merchants, attack him and throw him into a panic.

In Act II, scene iii, the action shifts to Hotspur, his wife, and the coming plans for revolt.

In scene iv, again we see the tavern at Eastcheap, a riotous scene in which the Prince tricks Falstaff into lying hugely about the number of attackers then reveals he knew that Falstaff was lying the whole time. Displaying his quick wits, versatility, and humor, however, Falstaff says that he knew that the attackers were Hal and Poins all along. What's extraordinary in this

a knight and a general and is ready to weep out of love, anger, and frustration with his son. He contrasts Hal with

scene is Shakespeare's use of language—mostly slang, often dealing with food and drink, delivered rapid-fire, and hilarious whether or not you know the exact meaning of the words.

Again, action shifts away from London to the North in Act III. Hotspur, Worcester, Lord Mortimer (last mentioned as captured by Owen Glendower) and Glendower himself are now in alliance against King Henry IV. In a cleverly worded quarrel, we see the two hotheads, Hotspur and Glendower—Hotspur a man of action, Glendower a visionary and, to our modern sensibilities, rather a madman. Mortimer and Hotspur say farewell to their wives, and the move toward open war advances.

In Act III scene ii, King Henry confronts his son Prince Hal, wondering if Hal's current behavior is part of God's curse on him for his sins. He recalls his own glory days as

Hotspur and even thinks that Hal would be willing to fight against his own father. Prince Hal ("God forgive them that so much have swayed/Your majesty's good thoughts away from me.") vows to "make this northern youth exchange/His glorious deeds for my indignities."

In Act III, scene iii, we see Falstaff with the hostess of the tavern, Prince Hal, and some of the "lowlives," showing how even the Prince proceeds from merriment to war. The scene begins with Falstaff talking about how he's aged, how he's

"fallen away" (gotten thinner—another lie from Falstaff), and how broke he is, but ends with Prince Hal's sending letters to his brother and the Earl of Westmoreland, because "The land is burning; Percy stands on high; / And either we or they must lower lie."

Falstaff would prefer to stay home and drink.

Act IV begins with Worcester, Hotspur, and Douglas and their civil

war. Hotspur speaks of the "nimble-footed madcap Prince of Wales," but is corrected as a knight describes Prince Hal's skill as a knight. In Act IV, ii, action shifts back to Falstaff, who has received orders to raise a company of soldiers. This is his opportunity to redeem himself, but he sees it as an opportunity to defraud the crown. Preparations for the battle to be fought at Shrewsbury continue in scene iii, while in scene iv, the Archbishop of York plots on his own to save his life.

Act V opens the climactic action. "How bloodily the sun begins to peer/Above yon bulky hill!" the king comments to Hal, Lord John of Lancaster, the loyal knight Sir Walter Blunt, Falstaff, and others. Vernon and Worcester, on Northumberland's and Hotspur's side, enter and go through the forms of attempting to resolve their dispute. "God befriend us," says the king, "as our cause is just."

In a series of scenes, we see the battle. Sir Walter Blunt, disguised as the king (one of several such body doubles) is killed by Douglas. Falstaff, terrified, promptly runs. Douglas attacks what he thinks is another stand-in for the king—but who is actually the King himself.

King Henry seems to be losing the fight when Prince Hal enters and drives Douglas away. "Thou hast redeemed thy lost opinion," the king tells his prodigal son.

Not a moment too soon, for now Harry Hotspur and Harry Plantagenet meet each other and fight, just as Falstaff finds himself confronted by Douglas. Instantly, Falstaff pretends to be slain. Meanwhile, the Prince kills Hotspur, an action he seems to regret—but not as much as the death of Falstaff. He goes off to attend to matters of the war, whereupon Falstaff rises quickly, drags Hotspur's body back to camp, and actually claims to have killed him. Prince Hal and his brother think that this is a fine joke, while Falstaff promises "If I do grow great, I'll grow less; for I'll purge, and leave sack, and live cleanly, as a nobleman should do." No chance of that, of course, as subsequent plays show.

The last scene consists of the King passing a sentence of death upon the surviving rebels and continuing the war, preparing theatergoers for the action that will occur in *Henry IV, Part II.*

QUESTIONS

•What do you think of Falstaff's ideas of honor? What's your take on the whole subject of honor, honor codes, personal honor, words of honor? Is this a concept whose time has come and gone? Do you see different types of honor within the play?

•In actual history, Harry Percy (Hotspur) was much older than Prince Hal—another case of Shakespeare altering history for the sake of good theater. Why do you think he did it? Does it work for you to have two young nobles of roughly the same age, rather than an older man and a young prince?

•Does anything in the play give you the impression that Prince Hal isn't the lowlife that he pretends to be? Do you see his character evolve? What about the highway robbery on Gads Hill? Is this proper behavior for a prince?

•To a great extent, the play is divided into aristocratic and rather "low-life" sections. Compare the historical scenes with those of Shakespeare's tavern crawlers, Falstaff and the others. What are the links between them? Do you think the final battle sequence works?

•Writers often say that some characters just come front and center and "talk" to them. They describe falling in love with their characters or having the characters take over. Do you think Falstaff was such a character for Shakespeare? Why or why not?

• In *Henry IV, Part 1*, the king for whom the play is named is pretty much overshadowed by his son. Discuss his role in the play and what motivates him. What do you think of his actions in deposing Richard II and in using doubles in the Battle of Shrewsbury? Are these actions honorable as you understand honor?

About the Essayist

Susan Shwartz holds a B.A. from Mount Holyoke College, and an M.A. and Ph.D. from Harvard University, and studied at Trinity College, Oxford, and Dartmouth College. She is the author of *Cross and Crescent* (December 1997, Tor Books); *Shards of Empire; The Grail of Hearts*; as well as two Star Trek novels (with Josepha Sherman); *Vulcan's Forge* and *Vulcan's Heart*. Five times nominated for a Nebula Award and twice for the Hugo, Dr. Shwartz has also taught at Ithaca College and Harvard University and has lectured at Mount Holyoke College, Smith College, Princeton University, West Point Military Academy, and the U.S. Air Force Academy.